THE MILITARY HISTORY OF WORLD WAR II VOLUME 15

EUROPEAN RESISTANCE MOVEMENTS

The Military History of World War II: Volume 15

EUROPEAN RESISTANCE MOVEMENTS

by Trevor Nevitt Dupuy
COL., U.S. ARMY, RET.

FRANKLIN WATTS, INC.
575 Lexington Ave., New York, N.Y. 10022

To Sarah

Library of Congress Catalog Card Number: 62-7382
Copyright © 1965 by Franklin Watts, Inc.
Printed in the United States of America

1 2 3 4 5 6 7

Contents

THE MILITARY HISTORY OF WORLD WAR II VOLUME 15

EUROPEAN RESISTANCE MOVEMENTS

Introduction—The Unknown War

THIS IS the story of a secret, almost unknown war. Yet for hundreds of millions of people during the years from 1939 through 1945 it was *the* war. Most of the fighters were ordinary men, women, and children who never wore a uniform.

The struggles of the conquered peoples of Europe against the Axis oppressors had very little effect upon the outcome of World War II. Even if all the conquered peoples of Europe had been docilely obedient to Hitler and Mussolini, the Allies would undoubtedly have won, but they might not have won as soon as they did.

Nevertheless, this Resistance movement was important in world history. It represented, in a very special way, the finest qualities of the human spirit. The history of the Resistance is the story of men who refused to accept tyranny, who were willing to die in an effort to bring freedom and peace to their loved ones even though the odds were often hopeless and, for many years, there seemed no possibility of victory.

The Land of Lidice

CZECHOSLOVAKIA

Abandoned and Betrayed

WHEN Adolf Hitler came to power in Germany, in 1933, he planned to make that nation the dominant power in Europe and to make himself the ruler of the greatest empire in history. The first part of his

1

plan was to bring all of Central Europe under German control. He knew that eventually he would have to fight powerful enemies in order to establish his prospective empire, but he believed that by taking little bites of territory at a time, he would at least be able to establish domination over rich and industrious Central Europe without having to go to war.

First he spent five years in building up a strong German army, navy, and air force. Then, in 1938, he seized the small country of Austria. Although the Treaty of Versailles (1919) had forbidden Germany and Austria to join together as a single German-speaking nation, none of the world's more powerful countries was sufficiently concerned by Hitler's aggression to do anything about it.

Only one European nation — Czechoslovakia — was really alarmed by Germany's annexation of Austria. Czechoslovakia was now almost completely surrounded by German territory. The little country had a fairly large, well-equipped, and well-trained army, but it was obvious that this nation of 12 million people could not stand up in war against 80 million Germans. The Czechs were confident, however, that if Hitler tried to seize their country, the Czech army could hold the mountainous frontiers long enough for their allies — particularly Britain and France — to come to their assistance. Soviet Russia also promised to help them in case of a German invasion.

The Czechs soon found, however, that nobody was going to help them. At Munich, on September 29, 1938, Britain and France agreed to let Hitler take the strongly fortified mountainous border regions of Czechoslovakia, which were largely inhabited by German-speaking people. The rest of the country now lay completely defenseless. But Britain and France promised to guarantee the new frontiers, so the stunned Czechs hoped that they could still survive as a nation.

On March 15, 1939, Hitler suddenly seized Czechoslovakia with overwhelming military force, just as he had taken Austria a year earlier. Again Britain and France did nothing. Czechoslovakia, abandoned by her friends, disappeared as a nation. The principal parts of the country, Bohemia and Moravia, became a German "protectorate," occupied by the German army.

The Early Resistance, at Home and Abroad

THE NEW RULER of Bohemia and Moravia was a German diplomat, Baron Konstantin von Neurath. He and Hitler soon discovered that they had extinguished neither the Czechoslovakian government nor the fierce, independent spirit of the people. The former Czechoslovak president, Eduard Beneš, had established a new government in London. Proclamations of this "government-in-exile" were circulated throughout Czechoslovakia by chain letters, right under German noses. A secret underground newspaper appeared, and a radio transmitter in England began to spread the word of freedom to the Czechoslovak people.

The Czechs at once made clear their contempt of the occupiers. When the Nazis issued orders that Jews could travel only on train platforms, the Czechs boycotted the railroads. Czechoslovak shops refused to serve Germans. In the movie theaters the people shouted and laughed and stamped their feet at German newsreels. They tore down German posters and placards or covered them with dirt. The people frequently assembled to celebrate national holidays.

At first the Germans were lenient, apparently expecting that the Czechs would soon realize that opposition was hopeless. Demonstrations continued, however, and the Germans began to take firm measures to prevent patriotic meetings.

The People Unite

OCTOBER 28, 1939, was the twenty-first anniversary of the founding of the First Czechoslovak Republic, and despite German orders, the people turned out to celebrate it. In Prague, the nation's capital, the peaceful demonstration turned into a riot when a German SS soldier* crushed the head of a nine-year-old boy with his rifle butt, simply because the boy was wearing a nationalistic emblem on his cap. A crowd immediately beat the SS man to death. This was the first of many bloody clashes between German soldiers and the aroused populace. The Germans imposed a brutal reign of terror, but still the Czechoslovakians refused to submit.

There were two main centers of the Czechoslovak Resistance. The first of these was the Czech Legion, veterans of World War I who had established the Czechoslovak Republic in 1918. Though these men were getting on in years, they were still fiercely devoted to their country. They were supported in their underground activities by the Sokol, a large physical-culture organization.

The Czech Legion and the Sokol did everything possible to interfere with the German war effort. They disrupted communications throughout the country, and committed acts of sabotage that slowed down the output of the German-controlled Czechoslovakian armament factories, the most modern in Europe.

One of the earliest exploits of the Resistance was the explosion of an entire department of a munitions factory in Policka. Eighty Germans were killed. The Gestapo intensified its efforts to break up the leadership of the Resistance, and in April, 1941, captured a number

---

* The *Schutzstaffel*, or SS, was the special military force of the Gestapo, the feared and hated security branch of the German Nazi government, which was led by brutal Heinrich Himmler.

Nazi concentration camp in Czechoslovakia. Translated, the sign over the gateway reads, "Work will make you free." Eastfoto

of leading members of the Sokol. The Gestapo then began to arrest factory workers and deport them to other countries in occupied Europe to work as manual laborers. The remaining workers responded by strikes, work stoppages, and sabotage. Mysterious fires kept occurring in the factories.

In July, 1941, the Resistance blew up a military train in an important pass in Slovakia. This held up railroad traffic during the early days of the German invasion of Russia, making it difficult for the Germans to get supplies to the battlefront.

Hitler decided that he must crush Czechoslovakian resistance at once.

Heydrich's Iron Heel

IN SEPTEMBER, 1941, SS General Reinhard Heydrich arrived in Prague to replace von Neurath as "protector" of Czechoslovakia. Heydrich was second in command of Heinrich Himmler's SS army, and head of the dreaded SD (*Sicherheitsdienst*, the secret police of the SS). It was he who had started the Nazi policy of exterminating all Jews in Germany.

Heydrich soon proved to the Czechs why he had become the most hated, and the third most powerful, man in Germany. In Czechoslovakia he declared a state of martial law. Any citizen found in the streets after dark was shot at once; hundreds of innocent people were executed; thousands were sent to concentration camps. Czechoslovakia became a land of terror.

Then, having given the people a taste of the whip, Heydrich set about winning them over. He began by granting favors to those who worked for the Germans. By means of radio and newspapers he told the Czechs how much he liked them. If they would cooperate with Germany, he said, he could help them.

The frightened, now thoroughly demoralized people were almost grateful to their brutal "protector." Only the bravest men continued to serve the Resistance movement. These patriots sent messages to the Czechoslovak government-in-exile, begging for help.

Great Britain, meanwhile, had established a secret organization known as the Special Operations Executive (SOE), whose mission was to aid Resistance movements in all the occupied countries in Europe. Working closely with the Czechoslovak government-in-exile, the SOE began to send trained Czech guerrilla fighters to help the Resistance in Czechoslovakia. Among the first to arrive were Jan Kubis and Josef Gabeik.

On May 27, 1942, these two men carried out a carefully made plan to assassinate General Heydrich as he was driving from his country villa into Prague. As Heydrich's car slowed to go around a hairpin curve, Gabeik tried to open fire with a Sten gun, but the gun jammed. Kubis immediately tossed a hand grenade. The grenade exploded in the car, and its fragments ripped into Heydrich's back. Gabeik and Kubis escaped, and a tremendous manhunt fanned out over the whole nation.

Heydrich died of his wounds a few days later. As a result, whole families were condemned to death on the mere suspicion that some of their members might have been among those who had plotted Heydrich's death. Then, following a pattern already made familiar by the murdered man, the Nazis postponed the death sentences in hopes that some frightened person would betray the guilty men. When the Czech people remained silent, hundreds of them were executed.

As pressure on their families increased, two members of the Resistance cracked and betrayed Kubis, Gabeik, and five companions. The seven patriots were discovered by SS troops in a church basement in Prague. During the daylong battle that followed, perhaps one hundred Germans were killed before a full-scale SS assault annihilated the defenders.

The Ultimate Barbarism

THE GERMANS suspected that some of the inhabitants of the mining village of Lidice, near the Kladno coal fields, had supported the Resistance group that had killed Heydrich. Kurt Daluege, Heydrich's successor, therefore ordered the complete destruction of the village on June 10. Every man was shot, and fifty-six women were also executed, while the remaining women and children were put into concentration camps. The Germans announced that "all buildings were leveled to the ground and the name of the village was immediately abolished."

Ten days later, despite the fact that Heydrich's murderers had already been killed, Daluege ordered that the town of Lezhaky should also be destroyed, and the little village, like Lidice, was wiped off the map.

The Germans were sure now that they had broken the spirit of the Czech people, but they had succeeded only in uniting the whole country in opposition, even though the increase in size of the German occupation force made active resistance much more difficult. Subversion and sabotage continued; the Germans were never able to make the Czechoslovak factories operate efficiently. There were no more dramatic incidents such as the assassination of Heydrich, however, and the Germans' brutal repression kept the people more or less under control.

Tragic Victory

IN 1944, as the Russian armies approached from the east and southeast, unrest in Czechoslovakia boiled more fiercely. An armed uprising took place in the mountains of Slovakia in late August. The Germans, though hard pressed at the front, combed the mountains and finally suppressed the uprising by the end of October. The Russians meanwhile had paused; they did not resume their advance into Slovakia until the Slovak and Czech partisans had been annihilated by the Germans.

In early 1945, however, the Russians advanced more rapidly until, in April, when the Germans again halted them in the mountains of

Moravia. The impatient Czechs in Prague decided to wait no longer and rose in revolt against the occupation force. On May 4, after several days of grim fighting, the Germans in Prague capitulated to the rebels and Czechoslovakia again became free.

The Czechs waited impatiently for the American Third Army under General George S. Patton to advance eastward from Plzeň (Pilsen), where the Americans had first liberated Czech soil on April 17. But Patton's advance stopped suddenly in the first week in May. An agreement had been reached between the Western Allies and the Russians, under which the Russians were to have the honor and privilege of occupying Czechoslovakia. On May 11 Russian troops arrived in Prague, where there was a great celebration. Even greater was the celebration five days later, when President Beneš returned to Prague to reestablish his government on its own soil.

It was not long, however, before the Czechs learned that they had merely exchanged Nazi tyranny for Communist despotism. Since 1948 Czechoslovakia has been a satellite of Soviet Russia, but the people who so bravely proved their love for liberty between 1939 and 1945 will certainly someday win back their freedom.

They Did Not Scare Us

POLAND

The Defiant People

THROUGHOUT their long and often sad history, the Polish people have demonstrated a special love of freedom and an unequaled determination to preserve their independence. They have also shown a

9

An underground army headquarters in Poland. United Press International Photo

fierceness in battle that has often aroused fear and amazement in their much more numerous German and Russian neighbors.

After their stunning victory over Poland in 1939, the Germans believed that they had at last crushed the Poles' spirits. But within six months, when the shock and despair of defeat had begun to wear off, small groups of Polish patriots began to forge a chain of resistance from village to village, from city to city, and from district to district. By the end of 1940 they had created a complete underground nation, administered locally without the knowledge of either the occupying German forces or the Russian forces who had invaded Poland from the east. This underground nation was in direct contact with the Polish government-in-exile whose headquarters were in London. In the face of the disaster that had overtaken the nation, Poland's many political factions were temporarily united.

An integral part of this new Polish underground state was a well-organized home army under the leadership of General Bor (Tadeusz Komorowski). The underground government also established its own courts and its own schools. It built secret munitions factories in city cellars, in deserted and isolated farms, and in any other place where a few people could work secretly to manufacture pistols, rifles, ammunition, and hand grenades. It even had its own police force, whose principal work it was to be sure that no traitors betrayed the growing work of the Polish Resistance.

The Jewish Combat Organization

FOR GENERATIONS the Jews of Poland had been discriminated against and forced to live in ghettos. Few joined their fellow Poles in the well-organized Resistance movement against the Russians and Germans. However, the Jews in the German zone in western Poland, where they were terribly persecuted by the Nazis, formed their own Resistance organization, with its center in the Warsaw ghetto.

Stalin, though temporarily an ally of Hitler, feared and hated Nazi Germany, and he decided to take advantage of Hitler's persecution of the Jews. Not only did he treat them well in the Soviet zone, but he also helped them secretly to evacuate other Jews from the Nazi zone to the relative safety of eastern Poland.

When the Germans attacked Russia in the summer of 1941, the Russians began to reap considerable benefit from the assistance they had given the Polish Jews in 1940 and early 1941. Through the Jewish underground they obtained valuable information about German movements and plans. Despite increasingly brutal persecution, the Jews sabotaged German lines of communication, directly helping the

German soldiers amuse themselves by cutting the beard of a Jew in Warsaw. Photograph from European

Russian armies in their desperate struggle against Hitler's invasion. In reprisal, the Germans began to arrest large numbers of Polish Jews — particularly in Warsaw. Many of these were sent as slave laborers to other parts of Europe. Others were shipped to the terrible concentration camps of Auschwitz, Belsen, and Buchenwald, where they were slaughtered by the hundreds of thousands.

Battle of the Warsaw Ghetto

THE JEWISH POPULATION of Warsaw numbered nearly 400,000 at the beginning of the war, but by early 1943 the Germans had reduced it to about 70,000. The Polish Jews began to realize that Hitler actually planned to exterminate all the Jews in Europe. Desperation often breeds spectacular courage. In April the Jews of the Warsaw ghetto rose violently against their German persecutors. Every single Jew — every man, woman, and child old enough to carry arms — became a soldier. For twenty-seven days — beginning on April 19 — these desperate people fought a brave but hopeless battle against the German army and SS units. Unfortunately, they had not coordinated their uprising with General Bor's Home Army. More than 13,000 Jews were killed, and over 50,000 captured. All but a handful of the prisoners were later executed by the Germans.

It is doubtful if Bor or his underground soldiers would have joined the Jews in their ill-fated uprising at this time. Bor knew that open and large-scale insurrection against the Germans could not succeed until Allied forces could give direct assistance. Furthermore, even though the Jews had cooperated with Bor's Home Army against the Germans, the fact that they had failed to cooperate against the Russian Communists (whom most other Poles hated) made Bor and his troops suspicious of the Jewish Combat Organization.

Never was resistance more courageous than it was in the Warsaw ghetto; never was it so hopeless. It is probable that the Jews knew they had no chance to succeed, yet one of the leaders of the uprising was able to write in his diary, as he saw the Germans approaching, "They did not scare us."

13

Warsaw ghetto in flames. Eastfoto

The Third Battle of Warsaw

MEANWHILE, General Bor and the other leaders of the Polish Home Army were slowly completing their plans for full-scale partisan underground operations. Late in 1943, as the resurgent Russians began to push the Germans back into Poland, the Home Army became active. Sabotage was more widespread, and better organized. Units of Polish partisans engaged German occupation forces in small-scale battles. The partisans struck swiftly and then disappeared into the Polish marshes or into villages and towns where they quickly merged with the remainder of the populace. In particular, the Poles concentrated against German lines of communications. They harassed rear-area troop concentrations, and did everything possible to assist the Russian advance.

Scene during the Warsaw uprising, 1944. Eastfoto

By the end of July, 1944, the Russian troops of Marshal Konstantin Rokossovski were actually in sight of Warsaw on the east bank of the Vistula River. The leaders of the Polish underground in Warsaw could hear the roar of battle in the distance. General Bor decided that now, in accordance with previously prepared plans for "Operation Tempest," was the time to initiate a final revolt.

The uprising began on August 1, when the Home Army seized large portions of Warsaw. To Bor's surprise, the Germans immediately counterattacked, showing that they had been expecting the uprising. It was also clear that the Germans were willing to undertake considerable risks by using all their reserves, even to pulling units back from the front lines, where they had been fighting the Russians.

15

Despite this German opposition, the Poles fought with traditional fierceness. In Mokotow, a residential district just south of Warsaw, a Polish unit was struck by elements of two or more German divisions in full-scale blitzkrieg assault. The Germans soon found out that these partisans were not just hit-and-run guerrilla fighters; they were first-rate soldiers. Although the German assault splintered the leading elements of the Home Army, the Polish commander counterattacked the German spearheads, then established a perimeter around Mokotow that repeated German assaults were unable to penetrate.

After a week of violent fighting throughout Warsaw, General Bor's army held about two-thirds of the city and its suburbs. The free world was electrified by radio reports of the uprising and its initial success. Every day official and private radio listeners were greeted by the haunting strains of Chopin's "Military Polonaise," as General Bor and his officers reported on the progress of the battle. There seemed no doubt that the German position in central Poland was doomed, since the success of the uprising made it inevitable that the Russians could quickly link up with the Poles to destroy the German forces in and around Warsaw.

But strangely, the Germans did not seem to expect this to happen. More and more German reserves were brought from all along the front, to be concentrated against Warsaw. By mid-August the German infantry, supported by an overwhelming weight of aerial bombardment, heavy artillery, and thousands of tanks, began to attack the insurgent positions. By the end of August the city of Warsaw was almost completely destroyed, and less than half of it remained in the hands of the Polish Home Army. Yet the "Polonaise" continued to be heard on the airwaves as the Polish rebels begged their allies to come to their assistance.

The Russian lines were strangely silent and immobile, though

British and American bombers began to assist the Poles, while American transport planes dropped supplies and munitions to the defenders of Warsaw. Stalin remained silent, even when Churchill pleaded with him to order his armies to advance. And the Soviets refused to permit American fighter planes to use Soviet bases east of Warsaw, from which they would have been able to give direct air support to the rebels.

Grandstand Seats for the Russians

THE RUSSIANS on the east bank of the Vistula River could clearly see and hear the terrible battle that was taking place in Warsaw, but still Rokossovski made no move. His long-range artillery, which could easily have struck the German positions in and around the city, was silent. Russian fighter planes, which could at least have hampered German air attacks, remained on the airfields they had refused to share with the Americans. Russian spearheads, which actually held a bridgehead over the Vistula River twenty miles south of Warsaw, did nothing.

After the war, Rokossovski insisted that in late July he had sent an urgent radiogram to General Bor Komorowski urging him not to start a "premature" uprising. General Bor and the other surviving leaders of the Home Army are certain that they never received any such message.

There will probably never be any actual proof of Russian intentions, but the facts are clear. The Russian armies, which had been steadily driving the Germans out of eastern Poland, suddenly came to a complete halt outside of Warsaw, letting the Germans direct all of their efforts against the insurrection. The verdict of history must be that Stalin deliberately permitted — if he did not encourage — the insurrection, even though he knew that without Russian help the Polish Home Army would certainly be destroyed by the Germans.

Even more suspicious is the fact that the Germans seemed to know that the Russians would not make any attempt to interfere. It is possible, therefore, that the Germans were actually notified that the Russians would not intervene.

After the war, other information came to light that showed that Russia's betrayal of the Home Army at Warsaw was only part of a Communist plan to get rid of the bravest and most patriotic Poles — the men who might support a free and independent Poland after the war.

In 1939, when Poland had been overwhelmed by both the German and Russian armies, the Russians had captured over 14,000 Polish officers, and these men later mysteriously disappeared and were never heard from again. In 1943 the Germans discovered a mass grave of many thousands of Poles in the Katyn Wood, near the Russian city of Smolensk. The Germans accused the Russians of having murdered these men. The Russians, in turn, accused the Germans of having massacred the Poles and of later blaming it on the Russians. During the war there was much doubt as to the truth of either of these conflicting claims, but later investigation makes it quite clear that it was in fact the Russians who murdered the Polish officers they captured in 1939. There could be no clearer proof of Stalin's determination to wipe out patriotic Poles who might oppose the communization of Poland after World War II.

As the Russians silently watched the Third Battle of Warsaw, the Germans continued their steady advance through the city, and on September 30, after the final "Polonaise" had been heard from Warsaw, the Germans overwhelmed the last insurgent stronghold, sixty-one days after the uprising began.

Three Polish patriots stand before a Nazi firing squad in Warsaw. Behind them lie the bodies of their companions, slain only minutes before. United Press International.

The Fourth Battle of Warsaw

NOT UNTIL JANUARY of 1945 did the Russians again start moving near Warsaw. Then, very quickly, they overran the weakened German units attempting to hold the ruined city. The remnants of the Polish underground, who now realized that the Russians were as much their enemies as the Germans, did little to help this Russian assault, which quickly surged across Poland and into eastern Germany.

The Warsaw uprising had greatly weakened not only the Polish Resistance organization, but also the Germans. It was easy for the Russians to win their final victory in Poland in early 1945. Thus, to the end, the Poles had unselfishly contributed to the Allied victory over Germany in World War II.

19

Sadly, however, the result was a Communist satellite government that for many years left Poland a virtual province of Soviet Russia. Today there is evidence that, despite all their efforts, the Russians have been unable to subdue permanently the Poles' fierce love of independence. The story of Polish Resistance in World War II, probably the greatest tragedy of modern history, may eventually have a happy ending, though that end is not yet in sight.

The North Countries

The Model Protectorate

TINY DENMARK was overrun by the German military machine on April 9, 1940. After less than one day of active fighting, King Christain X realized that further resistance would be suicidal. He therefore ordered his troops to surrender and urged his people to be calm and to cooperate with the occupying forces.

Hitler, encouraged by the rapid collapse of Danish combat resistance, and emphasizing the common Teutonic heritage of Germany and Denmark, attempted to make the newly conquered country into a model German protectorate. The Danish government was allowed to continue to run the country under the supervision of the military occupation forces; King Christian was treated with the honor and respect due a reigning monarch; the Germans made no attempt to introduce anti-Jewish laws. On the surface, save for the presence of German troops everywhere, things seemed normal and peaceful.

Danish patriots mount a barricade formed by an overturned bus in Copenhagen.
United Press International Photo

Yet, unknown to the Germans, within five days of the occupation of Denmark, the Danes had established an intelligence agency called "The Princes," which began supplying useful information to the Allies. The Princes kept close track of all German troop movements to and from Norway, and reported all German shipping movements in the Baltic Sea — particularly those through the Kattegat and the Skagerrak. At the same time a Danish newspaper correspondent in Stockholm, Ebbe Munck, set up his own intelligence service, which quickly made contact with the Princes in Denmark, and became the principal means of supplying the information to the Allies. Right under German noses Danish couriers, posing as businessmen or as newspapermen, regularly carried information from Denmark to Ebbe

Munck in Stockholm, who then sent the information on by radio and by airplane to Britain. Meanwhile, the Danish people surprised the Germans by refusing to accept them as "Teutonic brothers." The Danes made it clear that they felt only hatred and contempt for the Nazis.

King and Fuehrer

BY MID-1941 it was obvious to the Germans that it would not be easy to establish a model protectorate in Denmark. Slowly they began to increase their control of the Danish government, forcing the Danish police to carry out restrictive orders of the German army command. The Danes now demonstrated their hatred of their German conquerors by acts of sabotage. With the help of British SOE agents and Danish refugees trained in England, in early 1942 the local Resistance groups began to plan together for organized sabotage operations.

Hitler, however, still hoped that by retaining the friendship of King Christian he could persuade the Danes to join his European system. He little realized that Christian, even while he held himself aloof from any direct participation in the Resistance movement, was giving clear though unspoken support to the underground activities.

In October, 1942, Hitler sent a telegram to the King congratulating him on his seventy-second birthday. Christian acknowledged the telegram with a brief "thank you," which Hitler thought was cold and unfriendly. Deciding that there was no hope of friendship with the Danes, the offended Fuehrer broke off diplomatic relations with Denmark and ordered repressive army control over the country.

During 1943 there were frequent clashes between the Danes and the occupying forces, and more and more acts of sabotage. Finally,

Danish freedom fighters battle the Nazis. The man in front, wearing a German helmet, seems to be carrying an American carbine. United Press International Photo

led by their king, the Danes refused to comply with increasingly restrictive German demands. On August 29, therefore, the Germans imposed martial law, imprisoned all Danish military forces, and placed Christian X under guard. The Danish government ceased to function.

When the Germans were unable to find any leading Danish statesman willing to establish a puppet government, they established a military government. Immediately they changed the former policy of leniency toward the Jews and sent thousands to concentration camps — but the underground helped most of them escape to Sweden.

Active Resistance

SABOTAGE and harassing attacks against the German occupation forces now became even more frequent. The Danes established an internal Resistance army, following the Polish model. In June, 1944, the population of Copenhagen revolted peacefully against its German occupiers by staging a peaceful strike. As German troops poured into the city, the strike spread across the country. In response, the Germans cut off all public utilities in the city; but by July 3, with the Danes still on strike, the Germans agreed to a face-saving compromise that in effect granted the demands of the strikers. Most people returned to work, but the Resistance was intensified, and sabotage spread from the factories to the troop trains carrying German forces northward toward Norway.

In the closing days of the war, the Resistance seriously interfered with Germany's lines of communication to Norway. It also prevented the Germans from making full use of Danish agriculture. The resulting food shortage further hastened the collapse of Nazi Germany.

King vs. Quisling

NORWAY was invaded on the same day as Denmark, but geography and British naval interference, combined with the stubborn resistance of the tiny Norwegian armed forces, hampered the German conquest. After a struggle of two months, however, the remnants of the Norwegian army capitulated. King Haakon VII and his government fled to London, where they set up a government-in-exile. With British help, they immediately began to prepare a Resistance movement.

Meanwhile, a Norwegian traitor named Vidkun Quisling had established a puppet Nazi government in Oslo. For several months Quisling remained in control of the government, under German supervision. But when the Germans discovered that he was a weak and stupid man, with little support among his own people, Hitler sent German Reichskommissar Josef Terboven to Norway to become the actual ruler.

As in Denmark, Hitler hoped that by stressing a common Teutonic heritage and by treating the Norwegians as friends and favorites, he could win their cooperation. Quisling had assured him this would be so. Almost immediately, however, Hitler realized that the Norwegians were completely united in loyalty to their king, in hatred for the Germans, and in particular contempt for those few Norwegian traitors who had joined Quisling in the puppet government. The justices of the Supreme Court resigned, and most of them took key roles in the Resistance movement. On February 15, 1941, all eight Lutheran bishops in the country published a letter condemning German brutality and lawlessness.

The first important exploit of the Resistance was a raid from

British commando troops land on the coast of Norway under cover of smoke screens. They were assisted by Norwegian Resistance fighters. United Press International Photo

Britain against the Lofoten Islands, led by Captain Martin Linge, Norway's principal hero of the Resistance. During the spring of 1941, British agents and trained Norwegian refugees dropped by parachute to help organize an important Resistance base in the rugged mountain regions of central and northern Norway.

During the summer of 1941, the Norwegian Resistance was so effective that Terboven declared a state of emergency. This did little good. The Resistance celebrated Christmas by another damaging raid on Lofoten, and by the brief capture of the coastal town of Maloy from the German occupiers. During this action, Martin Linge was killed.

After February, 1942, Terboven used increasingly ruthless methods to try to maintain control of the country. He drove the Resistance

Oil tanks at Suelvik, on Oslo Fjord, blown up by Norwegian underground. United Press International Photo

completely underground, and captured, tortured, and shot many of its leaders. This only intensified Resistance efforts. In turn, German reprisals became still more harsh but could not stamp out the underground movement.

In response to Allied requests, the Norwegian saboteurs concentrated much of their effort on Norsk-Hydro, the hydroelectric plant at Lake Tinnsjo, where German scientists were making heavy water, an ingredient which could be used in the manufacture of atomic bombs. Allied intelligence feared that the Germans were making rapid progress in the production of this awesome weapon.

In February, 1944, when the first shipment of heavy water left Norsk-Hydro for Germany, starting on its way by ferry across Lake

Tinnsjo, Norwegian saboteurs blew up the boat and the supply of heavy water. There were no more shipments, because German scientists had decided that production of an atomic bomb was impossible.

In the spring of 1944, the Germans decided to try drafting Norwegians into the German army. They ordered a compulsory draft of all Norwegians of military age. Immediately the Resistance groups raided the conscription offices and destroyed all the machines and records.

Two months later, in July, the Nazis again tried to call up Norwegian men for their army. This time they promised the volunteers that they would get special ration books for themselves and their families. The Resistance promptly captured and destroyed the extra ration books. Instead of the 80,000 recruits the Germans had expected, there were only 300 reluctant conscripts.

As their defeat became inevitable in early 1945, the Germans prepared to destroy the archives that contained evidence of the few Norwegian traitors who had joined them and indicated which Germans had committed war crimes in suppressing the Resistance movement. Just before the archives were to be destroyed, however, the Oslo squad of the Norwegian Resistance dashed into the Department of Justice offices, seized the evidence, and removed it to safety.

On May 8, 1945, the Germans in Norway capitulated. The Norwegian Home Army immediately established control over the country, disarmed the Germans, and reestablished the legal government.

The Low Countries

Rejecting the "Master Race"

AFTER THE German conquest of Holland in May, 1940, the Dutch were confused, bewildered, and passive. Reichskommissar Artur von Seyss-Inquart felt that before long the Dutch would cooperate with their German cousins and become true Nazis.

To the majority of the Dutch people this was unthinkable. They could not forget that a Nazi air attack had needlessly destroyed much of the center of Rotterdam just before the Dutch surrender. Passive resistance began to develop throughout the country. At first this simply involved secret meetings of patriotic groups who hid weapons instead of handing them over to the Germans, distributed pamphlets, and generally prepared for an eventual Allied invasion.

Among the first of these groups to form was the so-called "Beggars Action," led by Bernardus Ijzerdratt of Schiedam. His plans called for a coordinated sabotage throughout the country. But before he could begin, he and most of his fellow leaders were captured by the Germans and executed in late 1940. Nevertheless, the Resistance movement grew steadily.

Early in 1941, the British Special Operations Executive sent agents to Holland to work with the local Resistance leaders in coordinating sabotage and in gathering intelligence data about German actions. By late 1941, the SOE–Resistance activities were going full blast, and sabotage was beginning to plague the Germans seriously.

"The English Game"

THE GERMANS realized that the Resistance had established a close connection with the Allies in London. The head of German military counterintelligence in Holland, a Colonel Giskes, working with the head of the Gestapo's department of counterespionage, Josef Schreider, established a project called *Englandspiel* ("The English Game"). During early 1942 their agents began to slowly work their way into the Resistance groups. As more and more German agents got into the movement, they began to take over posts of leadership and, pretending to be true Resistance members, made secret radio contacts with SOE headquarters in London. By May, 1942, the Germans had complete control of the Dutch Resistance movement. Although uncoordinated acts of sabotage continued, and while some Dutch patriots continued to help Allied prisoners of war escape through Belgium and France, for twenty months there was no really effective Resistance in Holland.

The Dutch and British Resistance headquarters in London did not realize this, and continued to send agents to the Netherlands and continued to receive replies in the proper code. It was about a year before the Allies suspected that something was wrong. By mid-1943 a few captured agents escaped and got back to England, to tell the SOE what had happened. The shipments of agents and materials to Holland were stopped immediately. A new Resistance support organization was established and, by the end of 1943, contact had been made with the few individual and uninfiltrated Resistance groups that remained in Holland. During early 1944 a new organization was slowly developed.

Low-Keyed Resistance

HOLLAND was too flat, urban, and densely populated, and too well connected by a network of excellent roads for true armed resistance against the occupiers. Sustained guerrilla fighting would have been hopeless. Thus, though there was a general will to resist among all of the Dutch people, there was no large-scale sabotage program or any actual armed uprising. Resistance was manifested by repeated general strikes, by assisting the escape of Allied prisoners of war, and by the collection of military intelligence to be radioed to London.

BELGIUM

A Suspect King

ON MAY 28, 1940, Leopold III, King of the Belgians, commander in chief of the Belgian army which had withstood eighteen days of terrible punishment by the most overwhelming and efficient military machine in the world, surrendered to Nazi Germany. This exposed the entire left flank of the French and English armies retreating toward northern France and the beaches of Dunkirk (Dunkerque).

Many Allies accused the Belgian king of treason and pro-Nazi sentiment. The Belgian government, which had fled to London, disassociated itself from the King's surrender and declared that it would continue the war at the side of the Allies, as a government-in-exile in London. With Britain's help, this government still controlled the Belgian Congo colony which provided valuable resources for the Allied cause.

31

Although some of his people and most of his allies in foreign countries continued to suspect Leopold of Nazi sympathies throughout the war, most of his people — and the Germans as well — quickly realized that he was no Nazi puppet. He refused to persuade his people to cooperate with the occupying force.

Friction began as early as the summer of 1940, when the Free University of Brussels rejected demands that would have made the university a hotbed for Belgian Nazis. Hitler, hoping to get Leopold to cooperate, invited him to Berchtesgaden in mid-November. Leopold was at first given red-carpet treatment, while being urged to collaborate with the Nazis. When he refused, Hitler berated him violently and sent him back to Belgium, to become a virtual prisoner in his palace at Laeken.

Confused But Successful Resistance

DURING 1941 Resistance groups were established throughout Belgium, but it was impossible to coordinate the activity of these groups because there were so many diverse regional and political interests and jealousies in the little country.

As German repressions and reprisals for sabotage and strikes grew harsher, street fights broke out in Belgian cities. Riots and sabotage led to more repression, and repression to increased resistance. Cardinal Van Roey forbade communion to all who approached the altar in the Nazi uniform. During all of 1941, the Free University of Brussels stood firm against German efforts to gain control and to make it an instrument of German and Belgian Nazi policy. Finally, in February, 1942, the university was closed by German orders.

During 1942 and 1943 strikes, sabotage, and sudden partisan raids against German guards and troop barracks continued. At the same time, a few of the Resistance groups gradually built up their strength and were loosely coordinated through the SOE. These groups began to develop effective military forces, using raids and sabotage activities as training exercises while they prepared themselves for active military operations when Allied forces should get nearer.

As 1943 turned into 1944 and German terror was intensified, the physical misery of the Belgian people increased, but their spirit remained unbroken. Then, when the news came that the Allies had landed at Normandy, the Germans transferred the King and his family from Laeken to Germany. The King's younger brother, Prince Charles, managed to evade the German guards, escaped on a bicycle, and joined the Belgian Maquis underground which had begun guerrilla warfare in the rugged Ardennes region near Spa.

The Partisans and the Allies

THE APPROACH of Allied armies toward Belgium in August and September gave heart to the Belgians and encouraged many to join the Resistance groups. The Germans, trying to reorganize after their terrible defeats in France, soon found it impossible to make a stand in Belgium because their lines of communication and their rear areas were being so severely attacked and mauled by the Belgian partisans.

An important Allied objective was to seize the port of Antwerp as quickly as possible, so as to make it a major supply base for operations against Germany. But General Eisenhower and his staff realized that the Germans would be likely to destroy the docks and machinery before the port could be seized. Radio messages were sent on ahead to the partisans to do all that they could to keep the port intact.

Plans for the protection of the port facilities were made by Captain Colson, a member of the National Royalist Movement of the Resistance, an intelligence group in Antwerp. Colson and his men carefully watched the German preparations for the destruction of the port. On the night of August 25-26, Colson's men destroyed most of the explosives that the Germans had assembled. Repeated sabotage of roads, railroads, and all enemy installations made it almost impossible for the Germans to move more explosives into the heart of the city.

Then, as the Allies came within sight of Antwerp, on September 3, Colson put his plans into effect. The German guards at the basins and docks were attacked and driven off before they could carry out their destructive missions. Explosive-laden ships, tied up to the docks, were seized and the fuses quickly destroyed. For five days there was heavy fighting in the port area between Colson's partisans and the remaining German guards, while the Allied troops battled their way into the city from the south and west. Finally, Colson and his men were also able to drive away the Germans attempting to flood the road tunnel under the Schelde River.

Meanwhile, in the city itself, Major Bauwens helped Colson carry out his mission by leading the main body of the Belgian Resistance force in attacks on German barracks and garrison installations to prevent them from reinforcing the dock area. Bitter fighting continued in Antwerp, even after Bauwens made contact with the first Allied spearheads on September 4. On September 7 German resistance ended, and the city was firmly in the hands of the Allies. By saving Antwerp and its port facilities from destruction, the Resistance fighters had contributed greatly to the ultimate success of the Allied cause in Western Europe.

A Tiny Nation's Determined Resistance

TINY LUXEMBOURG was overrun quickly, in early May, 1940, by the great Nazi armies that were rushing on to conquer Belgium, Holland, and eventually France; but although the defenseless state was easily seized, nowhere was resistance more determined than in this little country.

The Germans were surprised by the intensity of the Luxembourg Resistance movement. The country was Germanic in origin, and most of the people spoke German as their native language, so the Germans felt sure that the majority of the people would join them. Thus it was a shock to the Germans when, on October 10, 1941, they held a plebiscite to permit Luxembourgers to declare their intention to unite with the "Master Race," only to find that a mere three per cent of the people had any interest in joining Germany.

The pattern of sabotage and harassment of the occupying forces was the same in Luxembourg as in the other two Low Countries, although it was perhaps more effective in Luxembourg. Every conceivable type of resistance was carried out: sabotage, derailment of trains, strikes, "go slow" action, manufacture of shoddy war materials for the Germans, fund-raising for the victims of the occupation, encouragement and support for an underground press that kept the people informed of what was going on in the free world, and constant ridicule and harassment of the German occupation forces.

Peaceful little Luxembourg played its part in the final Allied victory.

35

Using an underground hideout deep in the woods, thousands of Luxembourg patri-ots evaded the Gestapo for four years, hiding by day and emerging at night to sabotage the German war effort. United Press International Photo

Rebirth of Glory

France's Darkest Hour

ON MAY 10, 1940, Hitler's military machine struck France and the Low Countries to initiate one of the most awesome demonstrations of military power in the history of mankind.

This was the third time in less than seventy years that a powerful German army had overwhelmed the frontier defenses of France; but in neither of the earlier instances — 1870 in the Franco-Prussian War, and 1914 in World War I — had either the French army or the French people recognized a frontier defeat as decisive or conclusive. Germany eventually won the Franco-Prussian War, but not until a revitalized France had fought the invaders to a standstill in an amazing vindication of both French honor and French military skill. And in 1914, after the bloody setbacks in the Battles of the Frontiers, the thought of defeat had never occurred to French General Joseph Joffre as he regrouped his forces for a mighty counterblow in the Battle of the Marne. The essence of French spirit was revealed in a famous report to Joffre from General Ferdinand Foch, commanding a French army engaged in that great battle: "My center is broken, my right retreats, the situation is excellent; I attack!"

In 1940, however, there was not one major French counterattack during six terrible weeks of combat. Only in two instances had an obscure French tank commander, Brigadier General Charles de Gaulle, attempted a counterattack. He had failed both times, after initial success, not only because of the overwhelming strength of the

37

Pierre Laval.

German army, but because no other French commander would attack at the same time.

French political leaders in 1940 were no more vigorous than the French generals. As the German armies smashed their way into the heart of France, a few brave men urged that the government move to North Africa, but the majority of French political leaders numbly accepted France's defeat. Old Marshal Henri Philippe Pétain, hero of the Battle of Verdun in World War I, was pushed forward as a figurehead leader by such defeatist and Fascist-admiring political leaders as Pierre Laval, to head the defeated French government and to beg surrender terms from Adolf Hitler.

The surrender became effective on June 22, 1940. All of northern and western France was occupied by the German armies, while a so-called "free" zone was left under nominal French control in southern France. Pétain established the capital of this shrunken nation at Vichy. The real leader of "Vichy France," Pierre Laval, ran a government that was completely under Nazi control. Never before had France or the French people surrendered not only their territory, but their honor as well, to a foreign invader.

A New Leader and New Hope

ONE MAN REFUSED to accept the fate which so many of his countrymen were willing to endure. This was Charles de Gaulle, the fifty-year-old tank general who had vainly tried to stop the German tide. When the Pétain-Laval government surrendered to Germany, de Gaulle climbed aboard the last English airplane leaving France for London.

In London, de Gaulle established himself as the representative of all "Free Frenchmen" who, like himself, refused to accept either the tyranny of Germany or the Fascist government of Laval. Through the force of de Gaulle's personality and ability, the Free French movement soon became a virtual government-in-exile in London, controlling several remnants of the French army scattered in colonial possessions throughout the world.

While de Gaulle was organizing his Free French movement, the British government established the Special Operations Executive (SOE). The support the SOE gave to the Resistance in other countries has been cited in previous chapters. The organization's efforts were particularly successful in its support of French Resistance movements.

De Gaulle, proud, touchy, irascible, and brilliant, was reluctant to accept British assistance. He wanted to keep his own activities in support of French Resistance separate from those of the SOE. He realized that France could never retrieve her honor and glory unless the French redeemed themselves. But he also realized that his pen-

General Charles de Gaulle reviewing a Free French commando unit in England.

niless government-in-exile could not effectively support the French Resistance movement without British aid. So his Central Bureau of Information and Action, while working independently of the British SOE, nonetheless closely coordinated its activities with those of the English, and worked cooperatively in the joint Allied effort towards the liberation of France and the defeat of Germany.

The Struggle Begins

WITHIN FRANCE, meanwhile, it soon became evident that a significant number of patriots still possessed those qualities of courage, resilience, and determination which had always distinguished Frenchmen. Only a few weeks after the terrible defeat, Henry Frenay, a young army officer, tried to arouse his stunned and lethargic countrymen. He established a Resistance group known as the Movement of the Liberation. Through his unswerving determination, the many separate groups were eventually joined together into a single, coordinated national Resistance movement, generally more effective than the similar movements in other countries of Europe. But this did not occur for many months.

The division of France into an occupied zone and a "free" zone helped the early organizers of the French Resistance. Despite some interference from the Pétain–Laval government, the underground groups in the unoccupied zone operated without fear of the efficient German counterintelligence organization in the occupied zone. By late 1941 the free zone underground movements finally merged into three separate organizations, known as Combat, Liberation, and Franc-tireurs (or Partisans).

The leader of the Franc-tireurs, Jean Moulin, former mayor of Chartres, became the outstanding figure in the struggle to unify the Resistance. In September, 1941, he went to London and obtained de Gaulle's support and assistance in his efforts toward this end. By March, 1942, Moulin succeeded in uniting the three separate groups there into the United Resistance Movement. (In French, the United Resistance Movement was called *Mouvement Unis Résistance*. Its initials spell the French word for wall, *mur*, and many people simply referred to the organization as MUR.)

The military organization of MUR was called the Secret Army; it was commanded by French General Delestraints, who took the name of Vidal. He organized and trained the Secret Army in preparation for support of an Allied invasion. Vidal's army was greatly helped by support from England; radios, military supplies, and military instructors were all dropped at night by parachute into the secluded mountain areas of south-central France where the Secret Army kept its headquarters.

In the north the Resistance groups arose almost as spontaneously as in the south, but German control of the region hampered their coordination and effectiveness. Nevertheless the many separate groups received considerable support from the British SOE and from Free French headquarters in London. Their sabotage activities harassed the Germans, and the underground provided London with useful intelligence information.

The Communists played little part in the early Resistance movement. But after the German invasion of Russia, in June, 1941, French Communists entered into the Resistance movement with enthusiasm and vigor. Their participation was welcomed by most French patriots who found themselves sympathetic with the Russian struggle against the Nazis, and who later admired the Russian success in stopping Hitler's invasion.

Although many Resistance fighters retained doubts about ultimate Communist aims and objectives in France, for the most part they accepted the Communists as hardworking, devoted, and effective

Remains of Nazi barracks blown up by the French underground. United Press International Photo

fellow fighters. A number of the best leaders and fighters in the French Resistance were either Communists or Communist sympathizers.

The Germans Strike Back

THE GERMANS were efficient and ruthless in efforts to stamp out the Resistance movement in the occupied zone. In the Vichy zone, where it was less effective, German counterintelligence worked closely with the Laval government and with the Nazi-dominated militia force which Laval used against the Resistance.

When American and British forces invaded the North African colonies of Morocco, Algeria, and Tunisia, in November, 1942, the Germans promptly occupied Vichy France. With all of France under their tight military control, they intensified their efforts against the Resistance movement.

At the same time, Moulin and Vidal began to recruit the various separate organizations which already existed in northern and western France to their central Resistance movement. But then the German counterintelligence force, assisted by a surprisingly large number of French collaborationists, began to take a heavy toll. In late June, 1943, both Moulin and Vidal were betrayed by traitors in their organization, and were captured by the Germans. Both men refused to give any information, even when tortured, and were finally killed. Weaker men talked, and on July 15 nearly all of the British SOE teams in Paris were caught and executed by the Germans.

Meanwhile, the Maquis, or guerrilla fighters of the Secret Army, had begun anti-German operations, particularly in the mountainous regions of south-central and southeastern France. Supported by increased parachute deliveries of arms and supplies from England, these Maquis bands were undaunted by the betrayal of their leaders and agents in Paris. The Italian army, too, tried to suppress the Maquis guerrillas in the Alpine foothills of southeastern France, but was notably unsuccessful.

The "Interior Army"

DURING THE latter part of 1943 and early 1944, the Maquis became more and more active and more and more effective in their operations. They successfully sabotaged German military activities and

Gas works at Marseilles destroyed by French underground. United Press International Photo

German transportation, and attacked all Frenchmen who were known or suspected to have collaborated with the enemy.

By this time, of course, the Allies were well along in their plans to invade northern France through Normandy. De Gaulle's Free French forces in England were a part of General Eisenhower's great invasion force. Eisenhower's headquarters prepared secret instructions to be sent to the Secret Army, now called the French Forces of the Interior (FFI). The orders could not be sent in advance, lest the Germans learn about the invasion plan through their spies.

On D day, June 6, 1944, the French Forces of the Interior received the long-awaited orders from London. Immediately the Maquis sprang into action. Under the command of General Pierre Joseph Koenig, they attacked German rear-area installations, blew up rail-

45

road lines, destroyed bridges, and generally interfered with the German war effort. General Eisenhower's SHAEF staff estimated that these FFI forces were the equivalent of five Allied divisions during the critical first days of the invasion.

FFI units in southern France also gave valuable help when American, British, and Free French forces struck the Mediterranean coast in late August. The FFI materially assisted in the siege and capture of German forces in Toulon and Marseilles, and in the Allied pursuit of the remnants of the retreating German armies up the Rhone Valley.

Victory in Paris

MEANWHILE General Eisenhower's forces had broken out of their beachhead in Normandy, and had begun a dramatic sweep across northwestern France. By mid-August they were approaching Paris, their advance greatly aided by the Maquis, who were hampering the German retreat.

On August 19 the FFI units in Paris, which until this time had limited themselves to quiet sabotage, went into open action. A full-scale battle spread throughout Paris. The German garrison fought back with typical German stubbornness and efficiency; but despite the disparity in weapons, the French Resistance fighters established themselves in several regions of the city and challenged German control. Units of the retreating German army, ordered back to Paris, were unable to stamp out the uprising. And in spite of repeated German counterattacks, the FFI held on to their scattered strongholds and, in fact, even began to widen their control.

Aware of the struggle going on in Paris, General Eisenhower hastened the Allied advance. But aware, too, of de Gaulle's feelings

A man and a woman of the Free French forces during the liberation of Paris. Note that she wears a captured German helmet, a German pistol, and has German hand grenades beside her. International News Photo.

Free French snipers during the liberation of Paris. United Press International Photo

General Charles de Gaulle parades in Paris under sporadic fire from Nazi and Vichyite snipers. Time-Life

about the need for a revival of French honor, he ordered American units to bypass the city, while only General Jacques-Philippe LeClerc's 2d Armored Division actually entered the city to join the FFI. With the main German armies shattered and racing for the German frontier, German resistance in Paris collapsed on August 25, as LeClerc's regular soldiers and the Maquis of the FFI swept through the city. De Gaulle arrived the same day and braved continuing German sniper fire in a triumphal march through the city on August 26.

By mid-September most of France had been liberated from German control. Parts of Alsace and Lorraine, however, remained occupied by German troops for several months, and the Resistance continued its activities in these areas; but for the most part the underground movement was now transformed into full-scale French participation in the Allied war effort. The small Free French forces that had taken part in the invasion became the nucleus of a new French national army that played an important part in the final victory over Germany early in 1945.

Thanks to Charles de Gaulle, and to the Maquis bands of the Resistance, France had recovered her honor.

Who Is the Enemy?

Instant Resistance

YUGOSLAVIA SURRENDERED to the Germans after ten days of combat in April, 1941. A few officers and men of the Royal Yugoslav Army, however, refused to lay down their arms, and fled to the mountains which cover so much of Yugoslavia. Among them was Colonel Draža Mihajlović, who established a headquarters in mountainous Montenegro, and became the core of an army of Resistance. By radio and by secret emissaries he kept in touch with the Yugoslav government-in-exile in London. That government promoted him to general and appointed him as its accredited representative in Yugoslavia.

Mihajlović and his tiny band then began to harass the Germans in the low-lying regions of Serbia. At the outset he was joined by the Chetniks (*četnići*), members of the official Serbian veterans organization. Many of these became full-time, well-trained guerrilla fighters, and some were secret agents in the German-controlled cities.

49

*Colonel Draza Mihaj-
lovic, leader of the
Yugoslav Chetniks.* In-
ternational News Photo.

Other Chetniks were in the home guards, and there were part-time
guerrilla units of older men who assisted the guerrilla bands at every
opportunity.

Mihajlović set up regional commands throughout Serbia and Montenegro, and in some other parts of Yugoslavia. His center of strength,
however, was in Serbia. The regional commanders, with local Chetnik units, worked under his control and guidance; they gathered intelligence, undertook sabotage missions, harassed German installations,
and organized informal political control over many mountain regions
in Serbia. While encouraging these activities, Mihajlović initially
refused to permit full-scale operations against the Germans, since
he felt such operations would be more effective in a general uprising,
to be coordinated with an eventual Allied invasion of the Balkans.

A Yugoslav guerrilla bayonets a Nazi in a farmyard. European Photos

This young Chetnik let his hair grow long, but it did not lessen his fierceness as a fighter. Colonel Mihajlovic's troops were credited with helping over four hundred Allied soldiers to get out of Yugoslavia. International News Photo

Rise of the Partisans

BEFORE THE WAR there had been a strong Communist Party in Yugoslavia. Although outlawed by the government, the Party had been secretly active in the cities, as well as in mountain hideouts throughout Yugoslavia, particularly in Croatia and Bosnia. The principal leader of the illegal Communist Party was Josip Broz — or Tito, as he was commonly known — who had spent many years in Moscow, and who had returned to Yugoslavia in the mid-1930's as a Stalinist agent.

At first the Communists took no part in the Resistance movement. But when the Germans invaded Russia, in June, 1941, they immediately took advantage of this existing underground network to begin their own Resistance activities against the Germans.

Tito organized what he called a National Liberation Movement, to which he welcomed not only Communists but also any Yugoslav citizens anxious to rid the nation of the hated German and Italian occupiers. Because Mihajlović and his Chetniks were already operating effectively in Serbia, Tito and his National Liberation Movement Partisans concentrated most of their efforts elsewhere in Yugoslavia — in Croatia, Slovenia, Dalmatia, and Bosnia.

By mid-summer of 1941 all of Yugoslavia was in flames, as Partisans and Chetniks — without any coordination — continued sabotage and outright attacks against the Germans. By the end of July, Mihajlović had cleared the Germans out of much of Montenegro, and soon after gained control of most of western Serbia. At the same time the Partisans in other parts of Yugoslavia were equally successful. The morale of the Resistance fighters, both Partisans and Chetniks, was high. Those in the forests and mountains knew that they held positions which the Germans could never capture without a major military effort. With the assistance of these mountain-based part-time guerrilla fighters, the patriots in the towns very successfully harassed the surprised and shaken German occupation forces.

The Internal Struggle

FROM THE BEGINNING, both Chetniks and Partisans feared and despised each other as much as they did the common German foe. Mihajlović and the Chetniks, successors and designated agents of the old Royal Yugoslav government, realized that Tito intended to establish a Communist government in Yugoslavia; Tito and his Communist Partisans, on the other hand, saw in the cataclysmic German invasion an opportunity to communize the whole of Yugoslavia. Mihajlović and the Chetniks obviously stood in their way, and Tito apparently put the destruction of Mihajlović even ahead of defeating the Germans.

Tito was a skillful and cunning politician, as well as a natural military leader. While doing everything he could to disparage the Chetnik efforts, he gave little or no hint to the non-Communist people in Yugoslavia that he wanted anything more than to defeat and drive out the Germans. He took advantage of Yugoslavia's old ethnic disputes, particularly that between the Serbs and the Croats, to arouse among his followers — Communists and non-Communists as well — dislike and distrust of the primarily Serbian Chetniks.

The existence of these two entirely independent and rival Resistance movements in Yugoslavia confused and worried Britain, as well as the United States after America entered the war. The British SOE and the American OSS (Office of Strategic Services) gave secret aid to both Tito and Mihajlović. Both organizations made numerous efforts to patch up the differences between the two rivals, but they discovered that compromise was impossible.

The man in the center, wearing no insignia on his uniform but displaying a red star on his forage cap, is Josip Broz, better known as Marshal Tito, in 1944. International News Photo

The Great German Offensive

HITLER WAS SO enraged by the successes of Chetniks and Partisans that he despatched reinforcements to the occupying forces in Yugoslavia, even though most of his armies were in Russia, or manning the coastal defenses of Western Europe. In late summer, 1941, the Germans began a major counteroffensive. By the end of August they had reconquered most of Montenegro, save for the most inaccessible mountain fastnesses. While this was going on, however, Mihajlović had established himself still more firmly in western Serbia. Hitler therefore decreed that Serbia should be restored to order by the most severe measures. German and Italian troops began to deal ruthlessly with the local inhabitants.

By this time the Germans realized the rivalry between the two Yugoslav Resistance movements, and they tried to play the two off against each other. In late 1941 the German commander in Yugoslavia seems to have persuaded Mihajlović not to interfere with German operations against the Partisans, in return for German agreement not to attack the Chetniks in Serbia. Mihajlović may even have given some assistance to the Germans in the offensive against the Partisans during November, December, and January. In any case, Tito has claimed that he was attacked by Chetniks at that time.

Tito and his National Liberation Movement survived the German offensive, however, and struck back successfully in a number of areas during the spring of 1942. At the same time Mihajlović took advantage of the German preoccupation with the Partisans to reestablish his control in much of Montenegro. Hitler again ordered his commanders to stamp out the Resistance in Yugoslavia.

In the spring of 1942 the Germans launched their third great offensive, partly against the Partisans, and partly against the Chetniks. They reoccupied most of the lowland regions in Serbia and Croatia, although the Partisans and the Chetniks retained their positions in the mountains. The Partisans, in fact, surprised the Germans by a counteroffensive which slowed, and in some places completely halted, the German drive. These Partisan successes led to further uprisings throughout Dalmatia, Croatia, and Slovenia. During the latter half of 1942, the uprising spread through western Yugoslavia, which was now almost free of German control.

During this period, Partisan propaganda stimulated widespread admiration for the Russians among the Slavs of the Balkans. News that the Russians were turning back the German invaders in their own country helped the Communists to recruit more adherents than Mihajlović, who had little success in recruiting outside of Serbia and Montenegro.

Yugoslav guerrillas, rounded up in the hills, are marched off to be executed by their Nazi captors. United Press International Photo

During the early months of 1943, the Germans, with Italian assistance, launched a fourth great offensive, this time concentrating their main efforts against Tito's National Army of Liberation. Once more they seem to have had at least the benevolent neutrality, if not the passive support, of Mihajlović and his Chetniks.

Again Tito retaliated by a major counteroffensive. The Germans were halted, and were seriously defeated on the Neretva River. This victory gained further popular support for Tito throughout Yugoslavia, even in Serbia and Montenegro, areas which had been previously devoted to Mihajlović. By the end of 1943 the Partisans controlled almost the entire coast of Yugoslavia from Trieste to the Albanian frontier. More than half of Yugoslavia was liberated, and most of this region was under Tito's control.

On November 29, 1943, Tito felt strong enough to renounce the old Yugoslav government and to establish his Council of National Liberation as the nucleus of a new Communist-dominated government. This forced the three major Allies — Britain, the United States, and Soviet Russia — to choose between the two rival governments and Resistance movements of Yugoslavia. The choice was not difficult for Stalin, who had already been giving full moral and propaganda support to Tito. The Soviet Union immediately recognized the Council of National Liberation.

The decision was not so easy for the British and for the Americans. Both of them continued to recognize the old government-in-exile, but also they recognized Tito's *de facto* government. It was obvious to

A German soldier searches a ragged Yugoslav guerrilla for weapons. United Press International Photo

In Tito's army women fought side by side with the men. Vera Krinzman (center right), only nineteen years old, was a heroine of the Yugoslav Resistance forces. United Press International Photo

them, furthermore, that Tito had enjoyed greater success than Mihajlović against the Germans. Communist agents in London made much of this fact, and convinced many Americans and British that Mihajlović was secretly collaborating with the Germans against the Partisans.

Allied aid to the Partisans began to increase, while that to Mihajlović declined. This aid greatly helped Tito to reinforce his ascendency in the Resistance movements of Yugoslavia.

In September, 1944, Churchill officially abandoned Mihajlović, to give full support to the Partisan movement. The Americans were slower to act, but they too finally abandoned Mihajlović, recognizing that, with the approach of the Russian armies to Yugoslavia, Tito would inevitably become ruler of Yugoslavia. American airplanes, like those of the RAF, dropped pamphlets urging all Yugoslavs to cooperate with the Partisans.

The Liberation of Yugoslavia

MEANWHILE, the bitter three-way struggle continued with mounting intensity in Yugoslavia itself. By the end of 1944, the Germans, despite their continuing offensives, held only a few cities and had sporadic control only over the principal roads and railroad lines. By this time Mihajlović's efforts were only a relatively minor part of a tremendous national movement, which was largely directed by Tito and controlled by his Communist organization.

Tito and the Partisans cooperated closely with the Russian armies that drove into Hungary in the fall of 1944. In the process, all of southeastern Yugoslavia was liberated, including the capital city of Belgrade, and was under joint Russian-Partisan control.

During the winter, with only minor Russian assistance, Tito extended his control over practically all of southern Yugoslavia. In early

The people of Belgrade, liberated from German rule, cheer the arrival of Soviet tanks. Sovfoto

1945, in coordination with the main Russian advances farther north, Tito's Partisans — now organized into army corps and armies — advanced through Dalmatia to gain control of all northern Yugoslavia except the small region of Croatia around Zagreb. After the German surrender on V-E Day, May 7, 1945, Tito quickly seized the remainder of the country. Later he captured Mihajlović, who was tried and executed as a "traitor."

The most successful independent Resistance movement of the entire war was that of Tito's Partisans in Yugoslavia. Although they received vital assistance from all three of the major Allies, the liberation of the country was nonetheless accomplished almost completely by the fighting men of the Resistance without the need for any organized military assistance. It was this success, and his great political and military skill, that gave Tito a unique position in the Communist satellite states of eastern and southeastern Europe after the war and enabled him to establish a government completely independent of Moscow.

Footnote in Albania

ALBANIA, a land of mountains and fierce independent tribesmen, had been attacked and conquered by Italy in early 1939, long before neighboring Greece and Yugoslavia fell to the Axis. But while the Italians had considerable trouble in controlling the unruly mountain tribesmen, there was no real organized Resistance movement in the

◄ *Baba Faya, leader of an Albanian guerrilla band, who left a Dervish monastery to fight the Nazis.* United Press International Photo

tiny country until after the Albanians realized that successful resistance was underway in both Greece and Yugoslavia. Encouraged by these examples, guerrilla bands became active in 1942, and were soon coordinated by the National Liberation Movement established by the Albanian Communist Party. From the outset this movement was dominated by Colonel General Enver Hoxha, the principal leader of the Albanian Communist Party.

At first this National Liberation Movement enjoyed the same kind of successes that were being gained farther north by their Yugoslav cousins. But the German counteroffensive in the winter of 1943-44, despite its failure in Yugoslavia, was quite successful in Albania. Most of the leading Communists were killed, and the Germans and Italians reestablished control over much of the country.

During the remainder of 1944, however, with assistance from the Allies and from Tito, the National Liberation Movement regained strength and once more established control over most of the country. In November, 1944, German armies withdrew from the country completely, and Hoxha established a government at Tiranë on November 29, 1944, with himself as prime minister.

The Cradle of Liberty

GREECE

Aftermath of Victory and Defeat

ONE OF THE GREAT accomplishments of World War II was the victory that the Greek army gained over the reckless legions of Mussolini when they invaded Greece in the fall of 1940. But when, in

April, 1941, Germany entered the war in the Balkans with blitzkrieg invasions of Yugoslavia and Greece, not even the active assistance of a small British expeditionary force was able to prevent the collapse of the overextended Greek army. Brave General Alexander Papagos surrendered on April 24, 1941, and three days later the last British units were evacuated to Crete and to Egypt.

The Germans and the Italians had little further trouble in establishing control over Greece. For several months the people of that embattled and impoverished country were too numb to resist.

Beginnings of Resistance

SINCE THE DAYS of Marathon and Thermopylae the Greek people have suffered many invasions, yet have always found some inner source of strength that has enabled them to fight and to regain their jealously-guarded freedom.

The spark that rekindled the flame of liberty in Greece was the German invasion of Russia in June of 1941. The Greek Communist Party had already established an underground subversive network throughout the nation, and they began immediately to incite resistance among all Greeks, both Communist and non-Communist. In September, 1941, they established a National Liberation Front (known as EAM) and a guerrilla fighting organization called ELAS, the Greek Peoples' Liberation Party. The principal ELAS leader was Athanasios Klaros, who began operations in the Roumeli region of northeastern Greece in mid-1941. Klaros was intelligent, able, and a born leader; he was also an utterly ruthless, cold-blooded, fanatic Communist.

But other Resistance groups had also begun to organize themselves throughout Greece. Several of these — some in Athens and some in the mountains — joined forces into an organization known as EDES, or the National Greek Democratic League. Their military leader was General Napoleon Zervas, a wise and patriotic soldier.

A number of smaller Resistance groups became active in late 1941 and early 1942. Important among these were "The National Band," commanded by a General Stepanos Seraphis; and EKKA, the National Party of Social Reconstruction, led by another professional soldier, Colonel Demetrios Psarros. The EKKA was the principal recipient of British military aid during the war.

Confused Conflict

It was only in the spring of 1942 that open resistance began in Greece. It started with a wave of passive resistance and sabotage in Athens that caused the Germans and Italians to close Athens University in May. Sabotage steadily increased in the cities, while the mountain guerrilla bands stepped up their activities. By the fall of 1942 the guerrillas had gained control of large areas in the more remote mountain regions of Greece.

Rivalries among the guerrilla units grew more intense, and many of these organizations devoted more time to fighting each other than they did to harassing the Axis troops. Monarchist groups were particularly opposed to the Communist-dominated ELAS. Even those groups whose sympathies were more republican than monarchical were opposed to ELAS, but somehow they failed to work together with any success.

The occupiers were unable to take much advantage of the disunity among the Greek Resistance groups. The wild and rugged mountains of Greece remained largely free; the Germans could really control only the lowland regions and a few roads and railroads.

The one important instance of close cooperation between any of

Greek guerrilla fighters in the mountains of Crete. United Press International Photo

the rival groups came on November 25, 1942, when EDES, under General Zervas, got the support of ELAS in a combined attack on the principal Axis railroad supply line into Greece. The guerrillas seized and destroyed the Gorgopotamus Bridge, but the Germans soon reopened it, and the Resistance never repeated this feat.

One of the most amazing episodes of the Greek Resistance movement came in March, 1943, when ELAS attacked the National Band and captured its leader, General Seraphis. The Communists gave Seraphis the choice of being executed or of becoming the commander in chief of ELAS. Not unexpectedly, Seraphis accepted the latter choice. Although he was not personally a Communist, he was a liberal republican and so was able to reconcile his own political views with those of the more radical Communists; and he became an effective leader of ELAS.

65

Greek guerrillas lined up to meet Canadian troops disembarking at Athens to reinforce British forces.

During the fall of 1943, and on into early 1944, ELAS tried to overcome all the other Resistance movements. It was only partially successful, however, because it could not operate against rival mountain stronghold any more effectively than could the Axis soldiers.

Victory as an Anticlimax

THIS STRANGE, many-sided struggle continued on into 1944. In October the Germans, having suffered disasters on other fronts, evacuated Greece. Georgios Papandreou, the prime minister of the government-in-exile in Cairo, returned to Athens accompanied by a small British force. Differences among the guerrilla factions soon led to outright civil war, which the British troops suppressed with difficulty.

Greece had been liberated, but the country was impoverished. The smoldering dispute between the rival guerrilla bands soon sowed the seeds for further civil war, which lasted until the Communists were finally defeated in 1949.

A Tragic Choice of Evils

THE SOVIET UNION AND THE BALTIC STATES

LITHUANIA, Latvia, and Estonia had won their independence from Russia during the Revolution of 1917-19. In the years between the two World Wars, the tiny republics were responsible, democratic members of the community of nations. The outbreak of World War II placed these Baltic states in jeopardy because they were located on the main sea and land avenues of war between Germany and Soviet Russia.

The pressure began late in 1939, after Russia and Germany had divided Poland between them. Soviet troops were concentrated on the borders of all three Baltic nations, and the Russian government demanded permission of them to establish naval and air bases on their territory. In hopes of preserving some independence, the three little countries agreed to the Russian demands: Estonia on September 29, Latvia on October 5, and Lithuania on October 10.

Then, in June, 1940, while Hitler's attention was on his invasion of Western Europe, the Russians again moved against the three small states. Accusing Lithuania of kidnapping Soviet soldiers, on June 14 Molotov presented her with an ultimatum demanding complete submission to the Soviet Union. Similar ultimatums were presented to

67

Latvia and to Estonia two days later. On June 17, one day before these ultimatums were to expire, Soviet troops occupied the three countries. Leading members of the governments escaped to the West, where they established governments-in-exile, while at home the nations were absorbed as integral parts of the Soviet Union.

While the people of all three of the Baltic states recognized that open opposition to the Russians would be suicidal, they were determined to try to regain their freedom if possible.

Lithuania

BY THE AUTUMN of 1940 an underground network had been established throughout Lithuania. Contact was made with the government-in-exile in London. An underground press kept the people informed and encouraged them to resist the orders of the occupiers as much as they could without provoking retaliation.

The outbreak of war between Germany and Russia on June 21, 1941, gave the Lithuanians hope. The underground Resistance movement immediately rose against the Russian occupiers, and on June 23 the insurgents proclaimed a provisional Lithuanian government. Most of Lithuania was liberated from Soviet control before the Germans arrived, and Lithuanian guerrilla fighters helped the Germans drive out the remaining Russians.

Lithuanian hopes of independence were dashed on July 17, 1941, when Hitler created a new "protectorate," Ostland, which included Lithuania, Latvia, Estonia, and White Russia. The provisional government was forced to disband; and the Lithuanians found that Nazi oppression was as intolerable as that of the Soviets. The underground network was reestablished, for the people hoped that Russia and Germany would fight each other to exhaustion and that Lithuania would regain her independence with British and American help.

When the Nazis ordered Lithuanians to register for enlistment in the German armed forces and for labor in Germany, the Lithuanians refused, despite all kinds of pressure brought upon them. They persisted in their determination not to join the German war effort.

In 1944, as the Germans were driven back, Russia again gained control over the little country. Once more the Lithuanian Resistance flared up against the Soviets, this time chiefly to remind the free world that Lithuanians were still fighting for independence.

Latvia

RESISTANCE in Latvia, first against Soviet, then German, control, was neither as well organized nor as effective as it was in Lithuania and Estonia. This was partly because the Latvians were more ruthlessly terrorized by the Soviets than either the Lithuanians or the Estonians. When Russian terror was followed by equally ruthless German control, the Latvians could see no reason to work for or against either dictatorship.

Through passive resistance, however, the Latvians showed a national solidarity that surprised and baffled both conquerors. From the few contacts that the free world still maintains with the Latvians, it is clear that this solidarity and hope for freedom still persists, as it does in the other two Baltic nations.

Estonia

RESISTANCE in Estonia was more vigorous than in either of the other Baltic states. When Russian troops first moved into the country in 1939, they were met by violent patriotic demonstrations which they suppressed ruthlessly.

Nazi death camp in Estonia. Hundreds of men, women, and children were shot or starved to death here. Sovfoto

The Russians deported many Estonians (as well as Latvians and Lithuanians), scattering them throughout other parts of the USSR — particularly in Siberia. They killed all those who had held any responsibilities under the free republic, and subjected those who remained to harsh repressions in every area of life. Thousands of the most patriotic Estonian citizens, under the leadership of former army officers, left their homes to take refuge in the forests and swamps of central and eastern Estonia.

When war broke out between Germany and Russia, these swampland refugees sprang into action, their ranks swelled by new recruits. They cut Soviet communications lines, attacked isolated Russian units, and seized great quantities of Russian arms and ammunition. Estonians who had taken refuge in Finland parachuted into the country with more arms and equipment. Except for a few of the larger cities, and some frontier areas where large Red Army contingents were concentrated, all of southern Estonia was under the control of the Estonian patriots before the Germans arrived. Many Estonians continued their fight alongside German units.

Estonian hopes of reestablishing independence were soon dashed by Hitler's colonial policy, which was savagely carried out by Alfred Rosenberg, Reichsminister for Ostland. The Estonians again went underground, but they were faced with the same terrible dilemma the other Baltic states had faced: effective resistance against the Germans might help the Soviets reestablish Communist control over the country; aid to the Germans in their war against Russia would merely insure the permanence of Nazi tyranny.

Nevertheless, the Estonians reestablished the Resistance in the hope of gaining freedom from either German or Soviet domination. The chief hope of the patriots was that, by demonstrating their will to resist, they could make Britain and America aware of their plight so that those two democracies would help them obtain independence at the end of the war.

This hope proved vain after the Russians reoccupied the country in 1944, but the Resistance groups continued to fight for freedom. They fought from the forests and swamps as late as 1947, and even today there are refugees in those swampland and forest regions who refuse to submit to Soviet Russia, and who still manage to keep in touch with friends and relatives in the free world.

The Ukraine

DURING THE Russian Revolution, and in the years immediately following World War I, the Ukraine became virtually independent of Russia, and a spirit of nationalism briefly flourished. But Stalin's oppression broke this nationalistic spirit in the late 1920's and 1930's. Before World War II the Ukraine was an integral part of the Soviet Union.

When the Germans invaded Russia on June 21, 1941, however, the spirit of Ukrainian nationalism flickered again. Communist commissars like Nikita Khrushchev immediately began a reign of terror to stamp it out, but were unable to do so before the German armies occupied most of the Ukraine in the summer and fall of 1941.

It is not surprising that in the early days of the war many Ukrainians joyfully welcomed the invading German forces as liberators. On the very day the Germans entered the city of Lvov, political leaders who had escaped the Communist terror formed a provisional Ukrainian government under Yaroslav Stetsko. And this independence movement spread eastward with the German advance.

Hitler, however, had no intention of establishing an independent Ukraine. He ordered the Ukrainian leaders to be arrested and deported to Germany, and claimed all the collectivized property owned by the Soviet state was claimed as Nazi war booty. In August, the Germans annexed the western Ukraine to Germany and turned the remainder of the Ukraine into a colonial regime under the vicious Reichskommissar Erich Koch.

The Nazis oppressed the Ukraine as severely as had the Russian Communists. They deported men and women to work for Germany — particularly those they feared might start agitating for Ukrainian independence.

This posed photo shows Russian guerrillas waiting for the German invaders. United Press International Photo

We can never know what might have happened if the Germans had encouraged Ukrainian nationalism, but it is obvious that the Ukraine — the richest farm region of all Russia — could have greatly helped Hitler's invasion. The German armies would have had no problem keeping open their lines of communication through the country, and their ranks would have been swelled by hundreds of thousands of Ukrainian soldiers anxious to preserve their independence by helping defeat Stalinist Russia.

But Hitler was not intelligent enough to recognize the opportunity. When the Ukrainians found that Nazi oppression was at least as bad as that of the Communists, they withdrew their support and friendship. A Resistance movement developed and, by 1943, a Ukrainian insurgent guerrilla army (UPA) was active under the skillful leadership of Taras Chuprynka. The UPA gradually gained control of much

73

of the rural Ukraine. The Germans concentrated their forces on the main routes and at the communications centers. Only occasional mobile detachments were sent through the countryside.

Armed resistance in the Ukraine was not confined to the UPA, however. The Soviet government sent many air-supplied Communist partisan bands into the area to operate behind the German lines. And although the Ukrainians had no love for the Russians, they preferred to cooperate with them rather than with the Nazis. Furthermore, the Communists assured the Ukrainians that when and if the Germans were driven out, the Ukraine would become independent and autonomous within a loose federation with the Soviet Union.

Taras Chuprynka and his UPA had never trusted Soviet propaganda and, as the Germans withdrew from the country, he and UPA began a war on two fronts: one against the retreating Germans, and one against the advancing Soviet army. Their position was hopeless, but the Ukrainian guerrilla fighters continued to resist. Bitter fighting in the remote country regions of the Ukraine continued until 1947, with many major battles occurring between the UPA and Russian forces.

Smaller-scale guerrilla warfare persisted at least until 1952. The UPA continues to exist even today, although there is no active fighting. An underground movement encourages the people to remember their former nationalism, and reminds them of Russian Communist oppression.

White Russia

LIKE THE UKRAINE, White Russia (or Byelorussia) was briefly independent during the Russian Revolution, and just after World War I.

Russian guerrillas are taught by a Red Army soldier how to handle a captured German automatic rifle. Sovfoto

But nationalism had never been as firmly developed in White Russia as it was in the Ukraine and the Baltic states.

Nevertheless, the outbreak of World War II and the German invasion were greeted by a majority of White Russians as a possible opportunity for freedom. But while the German military command announced it was liberating White Russia from Communist imperialism, Hitler and his Nazis really thought of White Russia as merely additional living space (*Lebensraum*) for the German people.

The White Russians at first believed the Germans' propaganda, and many of them cooperated against Russia. White Russian men volunteered to serve in the German army and were used by the Germans to protect lines of communications. Some White Russian units actually fought in the front lines beside the Germans.

75

But the Germans soon proved that they had no intention of granting independence. At the same time Russian Communist partisans, directed and controlled from Moscow, began to wage guerrilla warfare against both the Germans and the collaborating White Russians. The confused inhabitants of the sad country were faced with the same tragic choice as the people of the Baltic states and the Ukraine.

Many White Russian patriots withdrew into isolated country areas to organize their own partisan efforts against both the Germans and the Russians, but most of the people apathetically accepted the fact that they would be oppressed either by the Germans or the Russians, and offered little or no assistance to either side. Thus, the Byelorussian Resistance movement never developed any great strength. And as the Russian armies again moved westward into their country, with increasing Communist control of partisan activity in the German rear areas, the White Russian partisan movement was slowly crushed. By mid-1945 it had collapsed.

Georgia

THE NATIONALISTIC SPIRIT of the Georgian people, which had been demonstrated during the Russian Revolution and in the years immediately following, had been suppressed by years of heartless oppression by Stalin's government. Stalin was by birth a Georgian, but he seems to have been even more brutal to his own people than to others in his vast dictatorship.

As the Germans swept across central Russia and the Ukraine and approached the Caucasus, however, nationalism again arose in Georgia, and the Georgians welcomed the possibility that the Soviets would be defeated and the Communist regime destroyed.

As they charge through the burning village of Orlov, Russian guerrillas retrieve the weapons of fallen Germans and Hungarians. United Press International Photo

In early 1942 German agents helped to establish a Georgian Resistance movement. At the same time the Germans recruited Georgians from their prisoners of war and collected them into Georgian units, which were sent to fight against the Red Army. The Georgians did not fight for Germany because they loved the Nazis, but because they saw them as a means of destroying Soviet tyranny.

When the Germans dropped Georgian paratroopers near Tiflis in 1942, hopes rose higher, and the underground movement gained strength immediately. Anti-Communist and anti-Russian literature was circulated freely throughout the country. Armed bands took to the mountains, from where they carried out guerrilla operations aimed at disrupting Soviet troop movements and interfering with the flow of supplies to the battlefronts.

As German spearheads approached the Georgian frontiers in the summer of 1942, the people of Tiflis were called upon by the Resistance movement to overthrow Communist rule and to declare Georgia's independence. Insurrection became widespread, and the government lost control of much of the country.

But the German tide halted, and then ebbed, before reaching the Georgian frontier. As the Germans withdrew from the Caucasus, hopes of Georgian independence disappeared. Stalin stamped out the Resistance with his usual savagery.

Great Russia

WHEN THE German armies entered Great Russia, advancing toward Leningrad, Moscow, and Stalingrad, they still had an opportunity to take advantage of widespread Russian dissatisfaction with Stalin's Communist government. Many Russians would have been happy to help overthrow Stalin. The Germans, however, established a brutal occupation regime, and the majority of the Russians in the occupied regions, regardless of their own personal attitude toward communism, reacted favorably to Stalin's appeals for solidarity in support of "Mother Russia."

Before the war, the Communists had maintained tight control over the entire Soviet Union through three reliable organizations, which now provided a framework for an underground movement in the occupied areas. The most important of these was the Communist Party apparatus, controlled centrally from Moscow. Secondly, there was the Komsomol, or Communist Youth Organization, which was particularly effective in distributing patriotic propaganda among young Russians in occupied regions. Thirdly, there was the NKVD secret police force, many members of which remained in hiding, then

Germans capture a Russian guerrilla, disguised as a woman, who was dropped by parachute behind the German lines on the Novorossisk front. International News Photo

quickly reestablished radio communications with Moscow as soon as the German front lines had passed.

These three organizations, working closely together, established individual partisan warfare units, whose activities were coordinated from Moscow. The partisan activity included not only the operations of guerrilla bands in rural areas, but effective political activity to hold the allegiance of all the people.

A German blockhouse, protecting railroad line of communications, after having been captured and wrecked by Soviet guerrillas. Sovfoto.

Because of the unexpectedly swift German advance in 1941, and because many of the people were willing to listen to German liberation propaganda, the underground movement had little success at first. But by early 1942, with the German invasion clearly stopped outside of Moscow, the Communist underground in the occupied regions began to gain greater strength and greater confidence. Partisan bands began to attack German lines of communication, although mainly in rural areas.

Meanwhile the urban underground had two main tasks: psychological warfare against the Germans or any Russians who might be collaborating with the Germans, and intelligence operations to assist the main Russian armies. Both the partisans and the urban under-

This posed Soviet photo shows how Russian guerrillas fought German punitive detachments behind enemy lines. Sovfoto

ground employed sabotage and intimidation; but the urban groups, who were in closer contact with the occupying forces, specialized in assassination, terrorism, and in subverting and infiltrating both German and collaborationist organizations.

Women, children, and old men were used extensively as intelligence agents. The Jews, in particular, warmly supported the Resistance, since the Nazis were persecuting Jews in all occupied areas. It was, in fact, among the Jews that the Communists were able to establish the most successful counter-nationalist partisan units in the Ukraine and White Russia.

As the German tide receded after the Battle of Stalingrad, more and more Communist agents and leaders were parachuted into the occupied areas to improve coordination and to increase the effectiveness and efficiency of the partisan operations. Great quantities of weapons, radios, and other supplies were also sent by parachute. The advance of the main Russian armies was greatly assisted by the closely coordinated operations of large guerrilla bands, who maintained radio contact with the army headquarters.

The Russian Resistance was more efficient than any other movement in occupied Europe mainly because Soviet agents were more highly trained, and because the organizing was so thorough and without the rivalry which hampered other underground movements. By 1944 the partisan units in the German rear areas were arranged into competent divisions, corps, and even armies, keeping the German rear areas and installations in constant state of alarm, contributing greatly to the final German collapse.

A Word of Conclusion

THERE WERE three common threads in the anti-Nazi and anti-Fascist Resistance movements in the occupied countries of Europe during World War II. Two of these were bright threads; one was dark. One thread was the common yearning of mankind for freedom from tyranny; this was clear even in lands which had not previously known liberty — as in Soviet Russia — where men promptly tried to seize the opportunity to be free. Second was the great strength of nationalism, which helped to inspire men in their struggle for national independence as an aspect of their fight for freedom. The third thread was the pervasive efforts of international communism to take advantage of the war, and of the German tyranny, and to try cruelly to subvert the nationalist movements in the occupied countries in an attempt to replace brutal Axis oppression with equally ruthless Communist dictatorship.

These same three threads were equally evident in the Asian countries conquered and occupied by Japan. And, perhaps surprisingly, they appear as well within the European Axis nations themselves. How these threads were intertwined in these Asian and Axis nations, and how sometimes one and sometimes another became dominant in those nations, we shall see in a subsequent volume.

Index

85

年代	大事紀
1934年（24歲）	◎ 開始投入音樂創作，在日本創作或出版的作品，署名用「Bunya Koh」，這是以「江文也」的漢文姓名的日語語音，用拉丁字母拼寫，並按西方習慣書寫而成的。 ◎ 4月創作鋼琴曲《台灣舞曲》（作品1）（原名《城內之夜》）。 ◎ 6月7日、8日參加藤原義江歌劇團在東京演出普契尼的歌劇《波西米亞人》（今又譯《藝術家的生涯》或《繡花女》），飾音樂家蕭納德。 ◎ 8月參加東京「台灣同鄉會」組成的「鄉土訪問團」，返回故鄉台灣，在台北、新竹、台中、台南等地巡迴演出，擔任獨唱節目，並收集了民歌，這次活動對以後的創作有著深遠的影響。 ◎ 所作管絃樂曲《白鷺的幻想》在日本第三屆全國音樂比賽中獲作曲組第二名。 ◎ 創作女高音及室內樂《四首高山族之歌》。
1935年（25歲）	◎ 作鋼琴套曲《五首素描》，《十六首斷章小品》於次年7月完成全曲。 ◎ 完成管絃樂曲《兩個日本節日的舞曲》。 ◎ 完成管絃樂曲《台灣舞曲》（作品1）。日後以此成名之作進入國際樂壇。 ◎ 參加藤原義江歌劇團演出普契尼歌劇《托絲卡》。 ◎ 作管絃樂曲《第一組曲》、《節日時遊覽攤販》、《田園詩曲》、鋼琴曲《小素描》、《五月》、《鋼琴短品》、《五首高山族之歌》（為男中音及室內樂）、《大提琴奏鳴曲》、《南方紀行》等。 ◎ 管絃樂曲《盆踊主題交響組曲》，在日本第四屆全國音樂比賽中獲獎。 ◎ 美籍俄羅斯音樂家齊爾品在東京旅行演出，江文也直接向其學習作曲，歷時約一年餘。
1936年（26歲）	◎ 作《台灣山地同胞歌》（原名《生蕃四歌》），包括《酒宴之歌》、《戀歌》、《在田野》和《搖籃曲》共四首。 ◎ 隨齊爾品到上海和北平，研究中國民族文化及民間音樂半年之久。 ◎ 完成鋼琴曲《木偶戲》（又名《人形芝居》），由東京白眉社出版。 ◎ 管絃樂曲《第一組曲》在「現代日本作曲節」由新交響樂團演出，齋藤秀雄任指揮。 ◎ 完成鋼琴曲《十六首斷章小品》。 ◎ 在德國柏林舉行的第十一屆奧林匹克運動會上，管絃樂曲《台灣舞曲》在藝術競賽中獲賽外特別獎。 ◎ 東京白眉社出版鋼琴曲《台灣舞曲》；東京春秋社出版管絃樂曲《台灣舞曲》——這部作品之後並由曼佛雷德‧古爾立特指揮，日本中央交響樂團演奏，勝利唱片公司錄製唱片。 ◎ 台灣中部大地震，作《賑災歌》。 ◎ 合唱曲《潮音》（島崎藤村詩），獲日本第五屆全國音樂比賽作曲組第二名。 ◎ 完成鋼琴曲《三舞曲》、管絃樂曲《俗謠交響練習曲》、《賦格序曲》等。 ◎ 齊爾品在東京龍吟社出版江文也五部作品：鋼琴曲《小素描》、《五首素描》、《三舞曲》、《十六首斷章小品》、聲樂套曲《台灣山地同胞歌》，同時在上海、維也納、紐約、巴黎等地發行。 ◎ 作《第一鋼琴協奏曲》（作品16，雙鋼琴譜，手稿未註明創作年代）。

年代	大事紀
1937年（27歲）	◎ 管絃樂曲《盆踊主題交響組曲》由羅生·許塔克指揮，日本新交響樂團演奏，在東京日比谷公會堂演出。 ◎ 作長笛與鋼琴奏鳴曲《祭典奏鳴曲》（作品17）。 ◎《台灣山地同胞歌》、《祭典奏鳴曲》入選巴黎萬國博覽會演出曲目，並由巴黎廣播電台播放。 ◎ 為日本侵略性的影片《東亞和平之路》配樂，當時在東京寶塚電影製片廠擔任作曲。 ◎ 管絃樂曲《俗謠交響練習曲》獲日本管絃樂比賽獎。 ◎《賦格序曲》獲日本第六屆全國音樂比賽作曲組第二名。
1938年（28歲）	◎ 作獨唱曲《話流浪者之歌》（歌詞為日本現代詩作），發表於日本音樂雜誌《詩與音樂》創刊號。 ◎ 3月底，應北平師範學院音樂系主任、台灣籍音樂家柯政和之聘，自日本回國，任該系作曲與聲樂教授，從此定居北平。 ◎ 拒絕受聘北平敵偽組織「新民會」之職，但受託為《新民會會歌》、《新民會會旗歌》、《新民之歌》（前二者為新民會部長繆斌詞）以及《大東亞民族進行曲》（楊壽枏詞）等反動歌詞譜曲，為敵偽利用。 ◎ 開始潛心研究中國古樂、民間音樂和古典詩詞，在創作上進入一個新的時期。 ◎ 完成《中國名歌集第一卷》，内收《南薰歌》、《駐馬聽》、《春景》、《望月》、《紅梅》、《萬里關山》、《鋤頭歌》、《古琴吟》、《美哉中華》和《蘇武牧羊》十首歌曲，由東京龍吟社出版。 ◎ 由北京新民音樂書局出版《中國名歌》（十五首）。 ◎ 作鋼琴曲《北京萬華集》（後改名為《北京素描》），包括《天安門》、《紫禁城之下》、《子夜》等十首小曲，由東京龍吟社出版。 ◎ 完成兒童歌集《啊！美麗的太陽》，包括《美麗的太陽》、《好兒郎》、《勤學歌》、《莘莘學子》兒歌四首。次年，由北京新民音樂書局出版。
1939年（29歲）	◎ 完成混聲四部合唱曲《漁翁樂》。 ◎ 完成獨唱曲集《唐詩──五言絕句篇》（作品24），含有《靜夜思》（李白）、《春曉》（孟浩然）、《易水送別》（駱賓王）等歌曲九首，附有英文譯詞，配置鋼琴伴奏，由北京新民音樂書局出版。 ◎ 完成獨唱曲集《唐詩──七言絕句篇》（作品25），含有《楓橋夜泊》（張繼）、《黃鶴樓》（李白）、《江村即事》（司空曙）等歌曲九首，可謂《唐詩──五言絕句篇》的姐妹篇，同為北京新民音樂書局出版。 ◎ 完成管絃樂曲《北京點點》，以《十六首斷章小品》中的五首小曲為素材。 ◎ 完成合唱曲《清平調》。 ◎ 與北平女子師範學院音樂系學生吳蕊真（後改名為韻真）相戀。 ◎ 完成《宋詞──李後主篇》歌集（未編作品號），含有《離愁曲》、《教君恣意憐》、《春歸去》和《相思楓葉丹》等四首歌曲。 ◎ 完成合唱曲《南薰歌》、《萬里關山》、《駐馬聽》、《鳳陽花鼓》、《平沙落雁》、《望月》和《佛曲》等，由北京新民音樂書局出版。 ◎ 完成大型現代管絃樂曲《孔廟大晟樂章》，分〈迎神〉、〈初獻〉、〈亞獻〉、〈終獻〉、〈徹饌〉和〈送神〉六個樂章，引起樂壇注目。